HIDDEN PREPARATION

HIDDEN PREPARATION

Roszien Kay Lewis

CONFESSIONS
PUBLISHING

Hidden Preparation
Copyright © 2020 Roszien Kay Lewis
ISBN: 978-1-7359620-3-0

Printed and bound in the United States of America.

Editor: Erick Markley

Confessions Publishing is a subsidiary of Roszien Kay LLC, Lancaster, CA 93536

For information regarding discounts on bulk purchase and all other inquiries, please contact the author directly at roszien@gmail.com or www.roszienkay.com

AUTHOR'S OTHER BOOKS

Confessions of An Overcomer: From Tragedy to Triumph

Confessions of An Overcomer: The Truth About the Wait

Getting Spiritually Snatched

Surrender: Surrendering It All To Gain It All

Submit, Resist, Flee: Strategies To Living A Victorious Life

The Wilderness

CONTENTS

INTRODUCTION

~

According to the Merriam-Webster dictionary, hidden is defined as, "being out of sight or not readily apparent: concealed 2: obscure, unexplained, undisclosed." As you can see from its definition, to be hidden can be both a good or bad thing depending on the situation.

There are instances and situations in our lives where we possess a strong desire and/or urge to not be hidden. This can be for various reasons. In these instances, we want nothing more than to be exposed. We don't want to be in obscurity, not even for a second. We want to be seen by all who have eyes to see us. So, we fight against obscurity.

In some situations, this rebellion against being hidden may be okay. It may not cause anything bad to happen to us. It may not harm us. And even if it does result in us being harmed, the harm suffered won't be lasting. Because of this, we make a habit of fighting against being hidden over and over again until we are thrust out of obscurity.

The fight against obscurity becomes so embedded within us, that we carry this fight into our journey when walking with Jesus Christ. As we go through the process of transforming into the image of Jesus Christ, there will be moments when being hidden by God becomes an issue. Why?!? Because there will be times when we want nothing more than for us to be in the sight of others. All while God is trying to push us into obscurity. We want to be seen by those with the ability to see and those without the ability to see. But God has us hidden in plain sight. As frustrating as this may be, it's all for a bigger purpose.

The seasons in which God either hides us in plain sight or calls us into obscurity is all a part of His great and mighty plan that He has for our individual lives. Hidden seasons have more significance than you even realize! Hidden seasons are for our protection. They can help to fuel us. Hidden seasons can result in us decreasing in self-will and self-desire and to grow in God's will and His desires. They can literally cause us to be propelled into our next season in life. And they can help grow and foster our relationship with God!

No matter how you may feel about this season right now, my prayer is that by the end of this book, you will become fond of every hidden season that you'll be placed in. My prayer is that you gain a greater appreciation for it. And that you'll no longer see hidden seasons as a nuisance or a punishment; but you'll see them as a necessity.

Over the course of the proceeding pages, you'll be educated and equipped as you read about what men and women experienced during their hidden seasons.

CHAPTER 1:
HIDDEN FOR PREPARATION

⁓

Preparation: "the action or process of making something ready for use or service, or of getting ready for some occasion, test, or duty."

God will literally cause you to become hidden so that He can prepare you for what's to come. I liken this preparation period to the process a caterpillar goes through to become a butterfly. Their process, or life cycle, is known as a complete metamorphosis.

During their life cycle, they go through several stages. Each stage is extremely important. These stages are so important that if the caterpillar experiences trauma during them, it can result in deformity or even death.

STAGE 1: THE EGG STAGE

A caterpillar's first stage of life is the egg stage. During this stage, the female butterfly (the mother of the caterpillar) decides where she is going to lay the egg containing the caterpillar. What I love about this stage is that the mother butterfly is extremely intentional. She doesn't just lay the egg on the nearest leaf she sees or finds—Why?!? Because butterflies are very picky about what they will eat and different butterflies feed on different types of leaves (The Academy of Natural Sciences of Drexel University, "Butterfly Life Cycle").

The mother locating the optimal leaf to lay the egg on is very important. When the egg is hatched and the caterpillar emerges, it doesn't move from the leaf (*id*). Therefore, their placement needs to be one of safety that will allow them to grow and eat freely without risk of harm or annoyance (*id*).

FOR THE BELIEVER

For believers, this first stage is extremely important. Just like with the mother butterfly, this is the stage where God will place a believer in the place where they will be safe and able to eat! God, just like the mother butterfly, is extremely intentional. He takes into consideration everything too.

I know that you may be thinking how is this possible. How will He place me somewhere? I'm happy that you're thinking this. God does this by leading and guiding us to the place where He wants us to be through instruction. He can do this through placing a prompting, or unction in our spirit, that lets us know that the church where we may be visiting is or isn't the right place. Have you ever walked into a place and felt like you were at home? Or walked into a place and felt out of place? These are some feelings that you may feel that will let you know if the place you are considering is right.

Aside from giving you a feeling, prompting your spirit, or causing you to feel an unction in your spirit, God may also reveal whether or not a church is the place He wants you to settle through other means. He may reveal it to you in a dream, vision, or through someone else. When He does, you must obey Him.

A lot of times we decide to join a ministry ourselves without consulting God. As a result, we place ourselves underneath leaders that aren't capable of feeding us the "food" that we need. Despite popular belief, where you are "fed" the word of God is extremely important. And what you are "fed" is important too! We are living in a time when people are teaching sugar-coated or false doctrine (ideas that adds to, takes away from, contradicts, or nullifies the doctrine given in God's Word). This is why we must allow God to lead and guide us. This is why we must allow Him to "place" us where we need to be so that we will feed on what will nourish us.

STAGE II: THE LARVAL STAGE

After hatching, the caterpillar enters the larval stage. In this stage, the caterpillar silently eats and grows. The food that is eaten during this stage is stored and used by the caterpillar later as an adult.

As the caterpillar grows (100 times its size during this stage), its skin is unable to grow with it. As a result, the caterpillar makes new larger skin through the process of molting (this causes a growth hormone to be released that leads to the shedding of the old skin, so that the new skin that has developed underneath can be exposed). This process of molting occurs several times (*id*).

With each stage of molting, the caterpillar is thrust into a new stage referred to as an "instar." With each instar, the caterpillar's juvenile growth hormone keeps it from growing too fast. So, there is no danger of its body parts growing ahead of time. However, when the caterpillar reaches full size, its juvenile hormone declines until it finally ceases.

FOR THE BELIEVER

Similar to that of the caterpillar, there is a mandatory need for the believer to eat in order for them to grow! Without the consumption of the living Word—the Bible— the believer will not be able to go from being a "babe" in Christ, to a mature believer who is equipped to fulfill their assignments.

Another similarity between the caterpillar and believer during this stage is their "skin." As God gives the believer more anointing and revelation, there is a need for a "new" wine skin that is capable of holding them. The old skin that was once perfect before the surge in growth is no longer sufficient. So, God gives the believer a new skin that is able to contain them.

STAGE III: THE TRANSITION STAGE—PUPA (CHRYSALIS)

In the caterpillar's fifth and final caterpillar instar, its imaginal disc begins to emerge and finally grow (Butterfly School, "Metamorphosis). An imaginal disc is a sac-like epithelial structure that turns into the external structures of the head, thorax, lims and genitalia (Current Biology, "Imaginal Disc"). This growth is only able to take place as a result of the decline in the juvenile hormone and the surge in the growth hormone.

Once the caterpillar is full grown it stops eating. The pupa is usually suspended under a branch, hidden in leaves, or buried underground. It is during this stage that it is protected inside of a cocoon. It is also during this stage that the caterpillar's interior, which is a nutrient soup (Discover Wildlife, "How Does a Caterpillar Turn into A Butterfly?"), feeds the parts of it that are soon to emerge.

During this stage, it may look as though nothing is happening. This is far from the truth. It is during this time that major changes are happening inside. There is so much growth taking place. Cells that were present in the larva are now growing at a rapid speed. These cells are what will become the legs, wings, eyes, antennae, the sucking mouthparts (proboscis), and other important parts of the adult butterfly (The Academy of Natural Sciences of Drexel University, "Butterfly Life Cycle"). And the bulk of the caterpillar's mass is recycled into the adult features.

THE BELIEVER

There are times when we will feel as though we are placed in a cocoon like the caterpillar. From the outside it will seem like nothing special is happening to us. It may even appear to those who are on the outside that there is no growth or change happening within us at all. When in actuality this is far from the truth.

Just like the caterpillar goes through a period of being hidden while in plain sight, the believer goes through this too. During this time period, there is so much happening inside that will emerge later. What's happening on the inside is also a result of what the believer "consumed" during the time that they were eating. The Word of God that has been hidden in the hearts of believers, as well as the Holy Spirit, is what nourishes and feeds the believer during this stage. They are what is preparing the believer for the time of emergence.

Although there are some similarities between the caterpillar and the believer's process at this stage, there is a major difference. The caterpillar goes through this stage once in its lifetime. But the believer will go through this stage several times throughout life!

THE FINAL STAGE: THE REPRODUCTIVE STAGE (ADULTHOOD)

This final burst stimulates the emergence of the adult butterfly. The adult butterfly's job is extremely different from the caterpillar's. The adult butterfly's job is to mate and lay eggs until their death.

THE TAKEAWAY

As you can see, the preparation stage for the caterpillar and the believer is extremely important. There is absolutely no way that either one can progress into who or what they were created and destined to be without going through this hidden stage.

If and when you find yourself in this stage, embrace it! Enjoy it! And soak up and eat everything available to you!

REFLECTION SCRIPTURES

"And no one puts new wine into old wineskins. For the old skins would burst from the pressure, spilling the wine and ruining the skins. New wine is stored in new wineskins so that both are preserved."
(Matthew 9:17 NLT)

"And I am certain that God, who begun the good work within you, will continue his work until it is finally finished in the day when Christ Jesus returns."
(Philippians 1:6 NLT)

"Throw off your old sinful nature and your former way of life, which is corrupted by lust and deception. 23 Instead, let the Spirit renew your thoughts and attitudes. 24 Put on your new nature, created to be like God-truly righteous and holy.
(Ephesians 4:22-24 NLT)

"So all of us who have had that veil removed can see and reflect the glory of the Lord. And the Lord-who is the Spirit-makes us more and more like him as we are changed into his glorious image."
(2 Corinthians 3:18 NLT)

"If you keep yourself pure, you will be a special utensil for honorable use. Your life will be clean, and you will be ready for the Master to use you for every good work."
(2 Timothy 2:21 NLT)

CHAPTER 2:
HIDDEN FOR PROTECTION—JESUS

⟨≈⟩

There will be moments in our lives where God will send us into obscurity to protect us from the attacks of the enemy. During these times, God will use other people to execute His plan for our preservation. He will use their obedience to thwart, derail, and cancel the plans of the enemy.

A couple of years after the birth of Jesus, wise men came from the east to Jerusalem looking for Him (Matthew 2:1). When they arrived in Jerusalem, they asked king Herod the whereabouts of Jesus. They had seen Jesus' star and had known that He had been born. They were interested in locating Jesus because they wanted to worship the Messiah, the one that many had prophesied about and had waited for (Matthew 2:2). As soon as Herod heard what the wise men had to say, he, along with all of Jerusalem, were troubled (Matthew 2:3).

Herod was troubled because he was afraid that Jesus would take his position. He knew that the people had been waiting for the arrival of Jesus. So, he was afraid that Jerusalem, which he had taken by force, was going to be taken from him. He didn't want to contend with another king. Herod had no idea that Jesus was not going to contend with him at all.

All of the writings and prophecies that had been spoken about Jesus being King weren't references to the kingdom that was occupied by man. Rather, it referred to the kingdom that was not to be of this world—the kingdom of God. His error in thinking was due to the Jews' flawed belief that the Messiah would restore a temporal kingdom to Israel. The Jewish people, including Herod, assumed when the prophets wrote, " . . . for out of thee shall come a Governor, that shall rule my people Israel," (Matthew 2:6) it meant on earth.

This fear caused Herod to seek after Jesus. He sent the wise men to Bethlehem to search diligently for Jesus (Matthew 2:8). Herod lied and told them to let him know when they found Jesus so that he could worship Him also. Fortunately, God warned them in a dream that they should not go back to Herod (Matthew 2:12). So, instead, they went back to their own country after they located and worshipped Jesus.

After the wise men left, the angel of the Lord appeared to Joseph in a dream. He told Joseph to flee with the young Jesus and his mother Mary to Egypt. Joseph was instructed to stay in Egypt until the angel of the Lord told him to leave. The reason for this was because Herod would look for the young Jesus to destroy Him (Matthew 2:13). Joseph obeyed the angel of the Lord. He fled with his young child and wife at night to Egypt (Matthew 2:14).

Because the wise men had not returned as Herod had instructed them to, he felt as though he was being mocked. This caused him to send forth an order directing all children two years old and under to be murdered. Herod did this because he wanted Jesus dead but did not know exactly where he was. Herod was not going to allow another king to arise and take what he had: the kingdom!

Fortunately for Jesus, Joseph had obeyed the angel of the Lord before the slaughter of the innocent children occurred. He and His family continued to dwell in Egypt until the death of Herod. After which time, the angel of the Lord came back to Joseph in another dream. The angel of the Lord told Joseph to take Jesus and Mary to Israel (Matthew 2:19-20). However, when Joseph heard that Herod's son had taken his place, he became afraid to go to Israel. Thankfully, Joseph didn't have to go to Israel because God warned him against it in a dream. As a result of this warning, Joseph went to Galilee and settled with his young family in Nazareth.

As you can see, Jesus had to be hidden in order to preserve His life. Had Joseph not fled with Him and His mother to Egypt, He would have been among the children who were slaughtered.

THE TAKEAWAY

There are moments in your life where God will cause you to be hidden so that the enemy will not be able to kill you before you've matured. There are moments where He will cause what's within you to remain in obscurity so that those who would be threatened by what you carry won't be able to assassinate you.

When this occurs, you must understand that it's for your protection. No matter how uncomfortable it is, it will be according to God's doing. He will orchestrate things. He will set things in motion. He will cause others to do things that will result in you being protected also. So, don't despise these moments because it's for your good.

While hidden, you'll be able to grow and mature without having to worry about your adversary being on your tracks. You won't have to worry about being spiritually murdered before you're even allowed to really live!

When it's time for you to come out of hiding, God will let you know just like He let Joseph know it was time for Jesus to come out. Trust the process. Trust God's timing. Get comfortable until it's the perfect time for you to emerge!

REFLECTION SCRIPTURE

"But in that coming day no weapon turned against you will succeed. You will silence every voice raised up to accuse you. These benefits are enjoyed by the servants of the Lord; their vindication will come from me. I, the Lord, have spoken!"
(Isaiah 54:17 NLT)

"But the Lord is faithful; he will strengthen you and guard you from the evil one."
(2 Thessalonians 3:3 NLT)

"But let all who take refuge in you rejoice; let them sing joyful praises forever. Spread your protection over them, that all who love your name may be filled with joy."
(Psalm 5:11 NLT)

"For he will conceal me there when troubles come; he will hide me in his sanctuary. He will place me out of reach on a high rock."
(Psalm 27:5 NLT)

"He will not let you stumble; the one who watches over you will not slumber."
(Psalm 121:3 NLT)

CHAPTER 3:
HIDDEN DELIVERER

◈

The enemy is out to steal, kill, and destroy (John 10:10). As you read in the previous chapter, he will use whomever, even a king, to carry out his agenda. And he does this irrespective of the age of the victim. Just as Jesus had to be hidden for protection, Moses had to be hidden as well because he had been created to be used as a deliverer of his people.

Moses, who was born to Jochebed and Amram, lived in Egypt during the time that the children of Israel were slaves. He had an older sister named Miriam and a brother named Aaron. He and his family were from the tribe of Levi.

During their enslavement, and before his birth, the children of Israel grew greatly. Their growth in number caused Pharaoh to become afraid of them. As a result, Pharaoh spoke to the Hebrew midwives and told them to kill all male babies (Exodus

1:16). However, because the Hebrew women feared God, they did not do as Pharaoh ordered (Exodus 1:17).

As a result of the Hebrew midwives not killing the male babies, the children of Israel continued to grow in number. The people also grew mightier (Exodus 1:20). Because of this, Pharaoh told the people to throw the boys that had been born into the river (Exodus 1:22).

After this order went out, Moses was conceived and born. Immediately, his mother could see that he was a special baby, and she hid him for three months (Exodus 2:2). When she could no longer hide him, she made a little boat, placed him in it, and hid baby Moses in the reeds on the banks of the Nile River (Exodus 2:3).

Moses didn't stay there long because he had been rescued by Pharaoh's daughter (Exodus 2:5). Moses' sister Miriam had stood at a distance and watched her mother place him into the small boat. She also watched as Pharaoh's daughter discovered him. Once Pharaoh's daughter voiced her concern about not being able to nurse Moses, Miriam came forward and asked if she wanted her to assist. When Pharaoh's daughter told her yes, Miriam went and called their mother to nurse him for payment (Exodus 2:9).

Once Moses was beyond the time of nursing, his mother returned him to Pharaoh's daughter. From that moment on, Moses was raised as her own.

When Moses reached the age of maturity, he saw an Egyptian hitting a Hebrew. Moses decided to come to the Hebrew's aid and kill the Egyptian. After committing this murder, he hid the body in the sand. Moses had no idea that others had seen what he had done. It wasn't until a day later that he would find out when he intervened in a dispute between two Hebrew men (Exodus 2:13, 14).

Upon finding out that others knew what he had done, he became afraid. Moses fled into hiding as Pharaoh sought after him to kill him (Exodus 2:15). Moses lived in the desert of Midian for 40 years. While there, he became a husband and a father.

As Moses hid in the desert of Midian, he was stripped of the identity he had been given as a result of him being raised by Pharaoh's daughter. He was stripped of the security and prestige he had become accustomed to as a prince in Egypt.

His time being hidden in the desert was not a waste. God used this period to communicate with him. God used Moses' period of obscurity to prepare him for one of the greatest assignments—as deliverer of the children of Israel. Had Moses not experienced this period, he would not have been in a place to obey the Lord.

Remember, the Egyptians had their own gods. They did not worship who the children of Israel worshipped. Because Moses was reared by Pharaoh's daughter, it is safe to assume that prior to going into the desert of Midian, he knew nothing of, or did not serve, the God of Israel.

However, because of his retreat to the desert of Midian, Moses had become introduced to God. The people of Midian were distant relatives of the Israelites. They were descended from Midian, the fourth son of Abraham and his second wife Keturah.

One can only imagine the mighty transformation that Moses went through as a result of all that he was exposed to! We can only imagine how much uprooting of the idolatry of the Egyptians that took place within Moses during this time of obscurity. And the replacing of the beliefs of the Midianites.

We can infer that what Moses experienced and was taught, took root. We can infer that it was impactful because when the angel of the Lord appeared to Moses in the burning bush after God heard the cries of the children of Israel, Moses was receptive (Exodus 3:2-4). Moses instantly knew that it was God who was speaking. When God called for Moses out of the burning bush, Moses' reply was, "Here *am* I" (Exodus 3:4 KJV).

THE TAKEAWAY

We see from the onset of Moses' life that his hidden seasons resulted in his life being preserved. This is what happens during some of our hidden seasons. The enemy sends out an order to others to take our lives—this could be in the natural or spiritual realm—and God touches someone to preserve it.

When the Lord is not allowing obscurity for preservation, he allows it to remove our useless identity. Put another way, God will allow certain events to happen in our lives to drive us into obscurity, to strip us of the identity that we were given as a result of our upbringing and/or us following our own path in life.

We see this happening with Moses. It was necessary for him to go through the process that he went through during his hidden season as an adult. Why? Moses had to be stripped of the ideologies that had been placed upon him as a result of him living in Pharaoh's house, so that He could properly lead the children of Israel.

REFLECTION SCRIPTURES

"So be strong and courageous! Do not be afraid and do not panic before them. For the Lord your God will personally go ahead of you. He will neither fail you nor abandon you."
(Deuteronomy 31: 6 NLT)

"The Lord is good, a strong refuge when trouble comes. He is close to those who trust in him."
(Nahum 1:7 NLT)

"For you are my hiding place; you protect me from trouble. You surround me with songs of victory."
(Psalm 32:7 NLT)

"Though I am surrounded by troubles, you will protect me from the anger of my enemies. You reach out your hand, and the power of your right hands saves me."
(Psalm 138:7 NLT)

"So we can say with confidence, "The Lord is my helper, so I will have no fear. What can mere people do to me?""
(Hebrews 13:6 NLT)

CHAPTER 4: HIDDEN IDENTITY

~

There are times when the Lord will place you in obscurity to hide your identity. He does this so that He can use you in certain places and positions.

This is what occurred with Esther. After queen Vashti had been punished by being removed from being queen as result of her failure to obey, king Ahasuerus went on a quest to find a new queen (Esther 2:2). King Ahasuerus's servant suggested that he should request for virgins to be gathered and brought to the palace in Shushan (Esther 2:3). Where they would go through a process of purification under the supervision of his chamberlain, Hegai (Esther 2:3). Because king Ahasuerus was pleased with what had been suggested, he memorialized the suggestion in a decree and commandment and sent them out.

Mordecai, a Jewish man who lived in Shushan, received the king's decree. At that instant, he decided that Hadassah

(Esther), his cousin, whom he had taken and raised as his own after her parents died (Esther 2:7), would be among the virgins who would be brought to the king's house to the custody of Hegai, the keeper of the women (Esther 2:8).

Once in the care of Hegai, the fair and beautiful Esther pleased him (Esther 2:7). As a result, she received favor, which resulted in her getting her belongings, which were needed for purification, and seven maidens from the king's house. (Esther 2:9). Esther and her maidens were also given the best place in the house of women.

This was all done as she concealed her true identity. Prior to being taken to the king's house, her cousin/father, Mordecai, charged her to not reveal her people or her kindred (Esther 2:10). Mordecai did not want anything to get in the way of Esther becoming queen. Nor did he want her to be despised or face ill treatment as a result of it.

The charge given by Mordecai was not difficult for Esther to meet. No one asked her whether or not she was Jewish. Mainly because there had already been an assumption that because she resided in Shushan, she was a native Persian, not a Jew. Also, her appearance most likely did not show her nationality.

Although Mordecai had his reasons for giving Esther this charge, he was ignorant of the fact that the hand of God was in the concealment. He had no idea what was soon to occur. He had no idea that Haman's hatred for him would result in him plotting to kill all Jews. And he had no idea that their people would ultimately be saved because of what Esther would do!

THE TAKEAWAY

There will be times when God will cause you to experience a season, or seasons, of obscurity. In these seasons, your identity may be hidden from others. God does this so that He can place you in a specific place so that His will in that place, region, and area, can be carried out though you!

Had Esther not been queen, her and her people would have mostly perished as a result of the original decree that went out. Had she not been in that place and been willing to risk her own life by going in to see the king at a time when she was forbidden, the fate of her people would have been hanging in the balance.

It is an irrefutable truth that the queen was only allowed to go before the king after he called for her. This meant that Esther was not allowed to go before him just because she wanted to talk to him. Anyone who went before him without him requesting meant that they would be put to death. Esther, knowing what the rule was, risked her life by going before him without being called. But she did not allow the possibility of being put to death stop her. She was willing to risk it all when she obeyed her cousin and went before the king. As a result she was able to use her influence to ultimately save her people.

Just like God used Esther in this capacity, He will use you, even though you may be required to hide your true identity. Resist the desire to reveal who you are. Wait on God to reveal your identity at the perfect moment and time!

REFLECTION SCRIPTURES

"If you keep quiet at a time like this, deliverance and relief for the Jews will arise from some other place, but you and your relatives will die. Who knows if perhaps you were made queen for just such a time as this?"
(Esther 4:14 NLT)

"The Lord is a shelter for the oppressed, a refuge in times of trouble. 10 Those who know your name trust in you, for you, O Lord, do not abandon those who search for you."
(Psalm 9:9-10 NLT)

"Keep me safe, O God, for I have come to you for refuge."
(Psalm 16:1 NLT)

"Guard me as you would guard your own eyes. Hide me in the shadow of your wings."
(Psalm 17:8 NLT)

"Even when I walk through the darkest valley, I will not be afraid, for you are close beside me. Your rode and your staff protect and comfort me."
(Psalm 23:4 NLT)

CHAPTER 5:
HIDDEN TO REVEAL

~

There are times when God will send you into hiding after He has done something magnificent and powerful through you. When this happens, you may be left wondering if God had been pleased with your performance. You may even be left with your head spinning, feeling as if you've failed miserably.

When this occurs, you must understand that you being told to pull away isn't because you've done something terribly wrong, rather, it occurs because the Lord wants to show you more, so that He can use you more. And He wants to use different situations that you encounter during your hidden season to grow you in several areas—including your faith in Him.

The prophet Elijah was used mightily throughout his life by God. He is well known for the power that God had bestowed upon him to raise the dead, call down fire from heaven, cause the heavens to withhold rain, as well as render a barrel of flour inexhaustible. Elijah was a great man of power and miracles.

Prior to Elijah being able to be used to do all of these mighty things that he had done, he was driven into obscurity. After he had told king Ahab that the heavens would be shut up and there would be no rain (1 Kings 17:1), the word of the Lord came to him (1 Kings 17:2). The Lord said, "Get away from here and turn eastward, and hide by the Brook Cherith, which flows into the Jordan" (1 Kings 17:3 NKJV). He had literally been driven into hiding as he was preparing himself for ministry.

Elijah wasn't driven just to any place, he was driven to Cherith—a place that literally means "drought." A place where God would show himself mightily and provide for Elijah supernaturally. A place where God would show Elijah his miraculous power by having the ravens bring him bread and meat in the morning and evening (1 Kings 17:6). A place where Elijah was able to drink from the brook during a time where there was a drought.

He was shown God's grace and sufficiency during this hidden season. There was enough food and water for Elijah until God's purpose was fulfilled. Elijah had been shown the hand of God in a way that he had never experienced before.

During this hidden season, Elijah was able to go deeper in God and experience Him in a different way. As a result, he was stretched, his obedience was tested, and he was ultimately promoted from Cherith to Carmel. Ultimately, his hidden season worked for his good . . . it changed the course of his ministry forever.

THE TAKEAWAY

When God sends us into hiding byway of "Cherith," we must go if we are to grow and experience Mount Carmel. We cannot afford to miss this season either because there are so many lessons that God will teach us. These lessons will prepare you for what's to come. These lessons will cause you to trust God more, have faith in Him more, and understand His miraculous power and might on another level.

Below, are lessons that Elijah learned, that we can hold on to as we are being hidden before elevation!

1. **God will direct you** (1 King 17:1-3).
2. **God's promises are restrictive** (1 King 17:4)—In order to receive the manifestation of what God promised, we must be where God wants us to be. We must also do what God wants us to do.

3. **God's required prerequisites must be met** (1 King 17:5)—Elijah doing as God required, showed us that obedience is absolutely key. We must move without doubt, with no defiance, and with no delay.

4. **God will release provision** (1 King 17:6)—It was only when Elijah moved as God directed, and got to the specified place, that God released the provision to Elijah supernaturally.

5. **God's promise will be revealed in the end** (1 King 17:7)—After the brook dried up, God instructed Elijah to arise and go to Zarephath and dwell there, where he would be fed by a widow and be used for God's glory.

REFLECTION SCRIPTURES

"But Samuel replied, "What is more pleasing to the LORD: your burnt offerings and sacrifices or your obedience to his voice? Listen! Obedience is better than sacrifice, and submission is better than offering the fat of rams."
(1 Samuel 15:22 NLT)

"For I know the plans I have for you," says the LORD. "They are plans for good and not for disaster, to give you a future and a hope.'"
(Jeremiah 29:11 NLT)

"Once I was young, and now I am old. Yet I have never seen the godly abandoned or their children begging for bread."
(Psalm 37:25 NLT)

"Your word is a lamp to guide my feet and a light for my path."
(Psalm 119:105 NLT)

"So don't worry about these things, saying, 'What will we eat? What will we drink? What will we wear? 32 These things dominate the thoughts of unbelievers, but your heavenly Father already knows all your needs."
(Matthew 6:31-32 NLT)

"And this same God who takes care of me will supply all your needs from his glorious riches, which have been given to us in Christ Jesus."
(Philippians 4:19 NLT)

CHAPTER 6:
HIDDEN TO EQUIP—
APOSTLE PAUL

───────── ∿ ─────────

Seasons of obscurity can serve as some of the best equipping seasons of our lives. Let's face it, although we may be extremely intellectual and knowledgeable, there is still revelation that we can only learn by being in the presence of God. There are mysteries that can only be unlocked by communing with, being taught by, and being refined by Him.

God will sometimes pull us away from the noise of the world and the larger crowds to equip and train us for our individual assignments. He does this because He knows that being in obscurity is the only way that He will be able to properly equip us for the purpose He created us for. He knows that it is only during this time that He'll be able to truly prepare us to walk in what He desires for us.

We see this happening with Saul. Prior to his conversion on the road to Damascus, Saul had been persecuting followers of Jesus. He had done this because what Jesus had preached was contrary to what he had been taught. Saul was so deeply rooted and defined by what he had been taught by his mentor Gamaliel, that anything contrary was not acceptable. Because of this, Saul viewed Jesus and his followers as annoyances and rebels. This is why he persecuted them every chance that he had.

Little did Saul know, God had a great purpose for him. Little did he know that he was a chosen vessel, which would be used to bear Jesus's name before the Gentiles, kings and the children of Israel (Acts 9:15). Little did Saul know that he would have to suffer great things for Jesus' name (Acts 9:16).

Although Saul was ignorant of these facts, it did not stop Jesus' plan for His life.

Saul's view of Jesus and His followers was changed in one instant. As Saul traveled on the road to Damascus to persecute followers of Jesus, he had a life altering encounter with Jesus (Acts 9:1-5). Jesus blinded Saul and told him to go into the city where he would be told what he must do. Blinded, Saul did as Jesus required. Once in Damascus, Ananias laid his hands on the eyes of Saul.

Now converted, Saul wasted no time and preached Christ in the synagogues of Damascus (Acts 9:20). He preached Christ so much and with such power and revelation that the Jews in Damascus plotted to kill him (Acts 9:23-24). However, after spending a short time there, the disciples in Damascus could not allow this to happen. They took him by night and helped him to escape the wrath of the Jews by placing him in a basket and helping him down the wall (Acts 9:25).

Although many assume that the next place Saul went was Jerusalem, it wasn't, by Apostle Paul's own admission in the book of Galatians, he went to Arabia after God revealed to him that he would preach to the Gentiles (Galatians 1:15-16). You may be wondering why I mention this. I'm glad that you're wondering this. According to tradition, Apostle Paul would have had to be trained and equipped by the Apostles (the ones who were the disciples that walked with Jesus for three years) in Jerusalem.

But this was not the case. After God revealed to him what He wanted him to do, Apostle Paul did not confer with anyone (Galatians 1:16). Nor did he go up to Jerusalem (Galatians 1:17) to be trained and equipped by the apostles. Why?!?—God had a different plan for him: He wanted to equip and train Apostle Paul in the desert of Arabia!

This assertion is supported by Apostle Paul's own admission in Galatians 1:12 (NLT), "I received my message from no human source, and no one taught me. Instead, I received it by direct revelation from Jesus." Yes, the same Jesus that taught the Apostles, is the same Jesus that taught Apostle Paul.

Some have argued that Jesus did not in fact teach Paul, the Holy Spirit did. Although this argument is plausible because the Holy Spirit is the one that teaches us all things (John 14:26), I believe that Apostle Paul meant what he said. Why?!? Jesus had presented himself, not by way of the Holy Spirit, to Apostle Paul on the road to Damascus, but spoke to him directly and said, " . . . I am Jesus whom thou persecutest . . ." (Acts 9:5).

To further support Apostle Pauls' assertion that he had received revelation of the gospel he preached from Jesus, let's take a look at Apostle Paul's own assertion in Galatians 2:1-3, 6-8 (NLT):

"Then fourteen years later I went back to Jerusalem again, this time with Barnabas; and Titus came along, too. 2 I went there because God revealed to me that I should go. While I was there I met privately with those considered to be leaders of the church and shared with them the message I had been preaching to the Gentiles. I wanted to make sure that we were in agreement, for fear that all my effort had been wasted and I was running the

race for nothing. 3 And they supported me . . . 6 And the leaders of the church had nothing to add to what I was preaching. (By the way, their reputation as great leaders made no difference to me, for God has no favorites.) 7 Instead, they saw that God had given me the responsibility of preaching the gospel to the Gentiles, just as he had given Peter the responsibility of preaching to the Jews. For the same God who worked through Peter as the apostle to the Jews also worked through me as the apostle to the Gentiles."

How amazing is that? Pretty amazing if you ask me! Jesus took His time to pour into the one who persecuted His people. And He did it in a way that no one would be able to deny that Apostle Paul was with Him intimately!

After Apostle Paul emerged from Arabia, he did so properly trained and equipped. He emerged bold. He emerged strong and rooted in Jesus Christ. And he emerged ready to fulfill his assignment!

THE TAKEAWAY

We see from taking a glimpse into Apostle Paul's transition, that being pulled into a place where those who aren't familiar with us is for our good. It gives us a chance to commune with God. It gives God a chance to pour into us without all of the nonsense. It gives us a chance to become so intimately connected with our Savior to the point that no one will be able deny that we've been with Jesus.

The great things about this period is that you won't have to worry about those who doubt you. You won't have to worry about proving yourself or seeking the approval of others. You won't have to worry about being contaminated by what someone else knows. You won't have to worry about anyone besides the Holy Spirit shaping and molding you into who you were created to be!

REFLECTION SCRIPTURES

"Show me your ways, Lord, teach me your paths. 5 Guide me in your truth and teach me, for you are God my Savior, and my hope is in you all day long."
(Psalm 25: 4,5 NLT)

"For the Holy Spirit will teach you at that time what needs to be said."
(Luke 12:12 NLT)

"But when the Father sends the Advocate as my representative-that is, the Holy Spirit- he will teach you everything and will remind you of everything I have told you."
(John 14:26 NLT)

"For we are God's masterpiece. He has created us anew in Christ Jesus, so we can do the good things he planned for us long ago."
(Ephesians 2:10 NLT)

"But you have received the Holy Spirit, and he lives within you, so you don't need anyone to teach you what is true. For the Spirit teaches you everything you need to know, and what he teaches is true- it is not a lie. So just as he has taught you, remain in fellowship with Christ."
(1 John 2:27 NLT)

CHAPTER 7:
GOING AWAY TO SEEK GOD

~

All throughout the Bible, many went into obscurity to seek God. They would literally leave others behind to go somewhere alone to pray or commune with God. They did this a number of times throughout their life. What's amazing about these times is that either God showed up to speak with them, He sent one of His ministering angels, or He said nothing at all.

I believe that every believer should go into moments of self-imposed obscurity to seek God. Not only are these moments necessary, but they are extremely important!

Below are instances when Jesus went away to seek God.

"But Jesus often withdrew to the wilderness for prayer."
(Luke 5:16 NLT)

Throughout our Savior's life here on earth, He went away to seek God. During these times, He would send His disciples to another place so that He could have privacy as He prayed to God. He would also dismiss the crowd of people so that He could pray as well (Matthew 14:23). When he wasn't dismissing them, he would habitually withdraw from them to pray (Luke 4:42, Matthew 14:13). Jesus didn't care about losing followers or making the disciples mad, either. He placed seeking the Father above everything!

To say that Jesus placed priority on seeking the Father and praying to Him above everything else is an understatement. Before He made important decisions, He went to God. He also went off to pray to the Father when He needed to deal with the demands of ministry, grief—and preparing for the cross!

Jesus didn't care what time of day it was, either. Jesus would rise early in the morning while it was still dark and go to a desolate place and pray (Mark 1:35). When it was during the day, He would go to a desolate place and pray also (Luke 4:42). And Jesus went out to a mountain side and spent the night praying (Luke 6:12-13).

Although He was okay with praying with crowds of people, He also taught His disciples about the importance of praying in secret. He told them in Matthew 6:6 (NLT), "But when you pray, go away by yourself, shut the door behind you, and pray to your Father in private. Then your Father, who sees everything, will reward you."

THE TAKEAWAY

Jesus continually withdrawing from people, daily activities, and the demands of his ministry, to be alone with the Father shows us the importance of going into obscurity on a regular basis. He shows us that his ongoing intimate relationship with the Father was the reason why He was able to do all that He had done. It was the reason why He was able to have compassion, wisdom, and the power that He possessed!

The bottomline is this: if we are to truly be like Jesus, we must do as he had done while he was on this earth. We must go into obscurity and pray!

REFLECTION SCRIPTURES

"If you look for me wholeheartedly, you will find me."
(Jeremiah 29:13 NLT)

"Search for the Lord and for his strength; continually seek him."
(1 Chronicles 16:11 NLT)

"Keep on asking, and you will receive what you ask for. Keep on seeking, and you will find. Keep on knocking, and the door will be opened to you. 8 For everyone who asks, receives. Everyone who seeks, finds. And to everyone who knocks, the door will be opened.
(Matthew 7:7-8 NLT)

"I love all who love me. Those who search will surely find me."
(Proverbs 8:17 NLT)

CHAPTER 8:
HOW TO SURVIVE HIDDEN SEASONS

~~

A s you can see from the previous pages, we will all encounter hidden seasons. There is no way around them, either. Some hidden seasons are longer than others. However, it doesn't matter the length, or how often you may experience a hidden season, there are things that you can do to survive them!

You must survive and grow in every hidden season of your life. Why?!? Because there is great purpose in them. And you don't want to miss it, either. Below are some things that you can do to survive ANY hidden season.

1. **Recognize what season you are in.**
    It's very important to know the season that you're in, so that you will have a sense of what to expect. Although you won't be able to totally understand what God is

doing or what He will do in the end, knowing the season will give you an idea of what may happen.

2. **Don't fight against the season.**

   Fighting against what God is doing can cause you to be in a season longer than what God intends. Humbling yourself and allowing God to have His way will be a lot easier in the long run.

3. **Don't try to rush ahead of God.**

   There is a set time for everything to happen in your life. God's timing is perfect. He knows when you're ready to be released from your season of obscurity. Remember, He created the timeline.

4. **Ask God for guidance and direction.**

   We don't know everything. Our thoughts and ways are not like God's. He knows which way we should take. He's there to lead and guide us. Remember, He created the season, so He knows the path that you should take.

5. **Be fluid.**

   Don't get too comfortable with doing what worked for you in your last hidden season. God may be requiring you to do something different. Be willing to change when God requires it.

6. **Increase your prayer time.**

   Praying to God is the way that we communicate with Him. In prayer, He will give you the guidance you need.

In prayer, He will give you the strength you need to endure the process.

7. **Read the Word of God more**.

   Reading the Word of God will help to equip you. It's the Word of God that helps us to penetrate and tear apart any lies that the enemy will try to plant in our minds. Reading the Word of God will provide the Holy Spirit with another avenue to strengthen and encourage us during moments of doubt, fear, or uncertainties, while we are being hidden. It will also allow us glimpses into the lives of others who have survived seasons of obscurity.

8. **Set aside time to reflect.**

   You will need time to reflect on the things that are going on in your life during your hidden seasons. You can't just go through them without taking time to breathe. You may need to readjust in some areas. Take the time as needed!

9. **Trust the process.**

   While you are going through your hidden season, you must trust that it will all work in your favor. You have to trust that God is doing something amazing for you and through you. And that what He is doing can only be obtained, released, and manifested, if you go through it!

10. Obey God.

Obeying God may be one of the hardest things that you must do during your hidden season. Even though this is the case, you must do it. Obedience to God will result in your hidden season not extending past what God intends. It will also please Him in the end.

CONCLUSION

Seasons in which we are driven into obscurity can be God ordained or self-imposed. Each season of obscurity has a purpose greater than we could ever imagine. It's up to us whether or not we will take advantage of the opportunities of growth that we are given. It's up to us whether we will allow the Lord to process us. And whether we will allow the Lord to equip us.

Although while in the seasons of obscurity it can feel as though they will not end, they will. Although we may be scared out of our minds, we can rest in knowing that because God orchestrated them, He will protect us during them. As well as bring us out.

Next time, instead of fighting against your hidden season, embrace the moment and know that you will come out better. You will come out stronger. You will come out PREPARED!

BIBLIOGRAPHY

Aldaz, "Imaginal Disc."
Cell.org
http://cell.org (accessed October 30, 2020)

Butterfly School. "Metamorphosis."
Butterflyschool.org
http://www.butterflyschool.org (accessed August 10, 2020).

Jones, Richard. "How Does A Caterpillar Turn into A Butterfly?"
Discovewildlife.com
http://www.discoverwildlife.com (accessed August 2020).

The Academy of Natural Sciences of Drexel University. "Butterfly Life Cycle."
Ansp.org.
http://www.ansp.org (accessed August 15, 2020).

ABOUT THE AUTHOR

Roszien Kay Lewis — Juris Doctor, speaker and entrepreneur— is an emerging leader and catalyst with a prophetic voice. She has a deep rooted desire to see people healed, delivered, and set free. As a result she founded Destined to Be Released Ministries, a ministry whose sole objective is to encourage, teach, and equip others through the Word of God. Roszien has hosted conferences, workshops, and spearheads the "21 Day Jump Start My Draw" prayer challenge.

As a result of the trauma she suffered in her childhood and teenage years, Roszien formed #ConfessionsOfAnOvercomer motivational speaking company. Through this company she shares her testimony of overcoming every obstacle in her life. And she encourages others that they too can overcome anything as long as they believe in themselves.

When Roszien is not ministering to or mentoring others, she's busy assisting others with book publishing. She is the sole owner of Confessions Publishing, a Christian based publishing company that assists authors with "turning their manuscripts into a masterpiece."

Roszien resides in California with her two beautiful daughters, Aaliyah and Myah.

CONTACT ROSZIEN

FACEBOOK: ROSZIEN KAY LEWIS

IG: ROSZIEN KAY LEWIS

EMAIL: roszien@gmail.com

Website : Roszienkay.com

www.ingramcontent.com/pod-product-compliance
Lightning Source LLC
Chambersburg PA
CBHW022129280326
41933CB00007B/614